CELEBRATION LIGHTS

Revealing the Mystery of Jesus and Hanukkah

STORY BY
MELODY HOPE

POEM BY ANN SEVERANCE

ILLUSTRATIONS BY
LAURIE WONG

Celebration Lights

Copyright © 2022 Tikvah Publishing

All Rights Reserved. No part of this publication may be reproduced, stored in a retrieval system, or transmitted in any form or by any means—electronic, mechanical, photocopy, recording, or any other—except for brief quotations in printed reviews, without the prior permission of the publisher.

For further information, please contact the publisher:

Tikvah Publishing

Joanie@JoanMasterson.com

ISBN: 978-1-63173-080-1

Published October 18, 2022

Printed in the United States of America

Editor: Ann Severance, annwsev@att.net
Production: Melissa Staff

Jewish families have high regard
for passing down to their children
the legacy of the word of God
given to them by the
God of Abraham, Isaac, and Jacob.

I trust this book will also become
a family treasure to pass down
to the generations
so they will come to know the mysteries
of Jesus in the Hanukkah story.

Every good gift and every perfect gift
is from above and comes down
from the Father of lights, with whom
there is no variation or shadow of turning.

— James 1:17 NKJV

Jeremy could hardly wait until mom shut off the car motor.

He ran into the house to tell his grandmother about how much fun he had with his friend Caleb.

"Grandma, Grandma, Where are you?" called Jeremy.

"I'm here in the family room, Jeremy," Grandma called back.

Jeremy emptied his pockets and dropped chocolate candy coins and a little wooden top into Grandma's lap. "Grandma, look at what Caleb gave me."

Grandma smiled and said, "Jeremy, I had a top just like that when I was your age. Did Caleb tell you how to play with it? I have forgotten the rules."

"Yes Gram, he told me the top is called a dreidel and the chocolate candy money is called gelt. See, there is a letter on each side of the top.

"Did he tell you the names of the letters and what they mean?"

"Yes, he did, and Mrs. Katz gave me a paper with the letters to help me remember how to play when I bring the dreidel home.

"Mrs. Katz told me the letters are the first letter of the words that make up the sentence 'A great miracle happened there!'"

"Did she tell you, Jeremy, what the miracle was?"

"Yes, Caleb's mom read us a story about it. She gave us a book about Hanukkah to bring home, too. Can you read it to me again?"

"Sure," said Grandma. "That can be our bedtime story tonight."

"Hi, Mom, how was your day?" asked Jeremy's mom as she came into the family room.

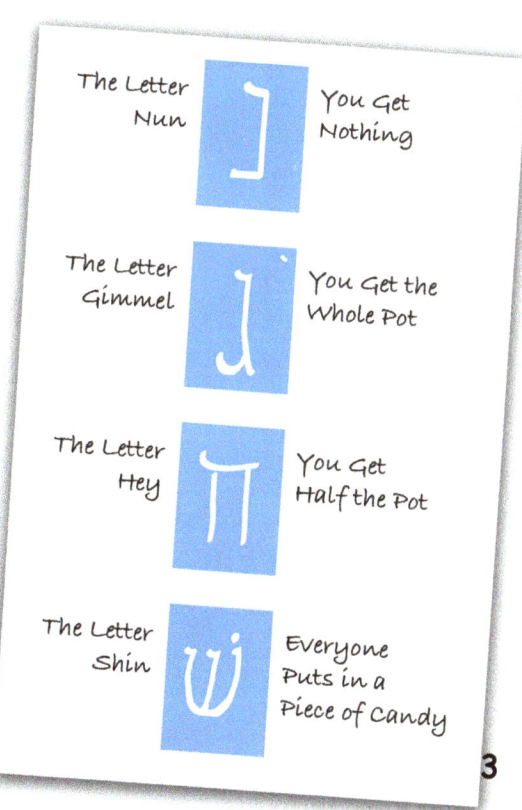

"I had a good day, honey. Did you enjoy your visit with the Katzes?"

"We had a lovely time celebrating Hanukkah. She was so kind and gave us this Hanukkiah," she said, holding it up. "It is a very special candle holder, used only during this celebration. She also gave us a book about Hanukkah . . . oh, and some yummy donuts!"

"This Hanukkiah holds nine candles, but Mrs. Katz said some burn oil," Jeremy chimed in. "You have a lamp that burns oil, don't you, Grandma?"

"Yes, mine is called a menorah. The menorah has seven branches, like the one they used in the Temple during Bible days. I use it for Shabbat, the weekly Jewish day of rest. The seven branches also hold candles, although I like to burn oil," she explained. She reached out to touch the Hanukkiah. "Oh, this is beautiful, and I can't wait to read the book tonight at bedtime, Jeremy!"

Jeremy grinned in anticipation. "Mrs. Katz told us they celebrate for eight days and light the candles each night. Caleb let me light some tonight while he said the prayer in Hebrew. He told me Hebrew is the language the Jewish people speak." He paused and turned to his grandmother. "Grandma, do you speak Hebrew?"

She sighed. "Sadly, I know only a few prayers in Hebrew that I learned as a child. Now I wish I had paid better attention."

"Look, Gram, this Hanukkiah has nine candleholders. The tallest candle in the middle—the one I used to light the other candles—is called the Shamash. Caleb told me that's a Hebrew word that means 'helper' in English. Guess I was a Shamash, too, because I 'helped' him celebrate Hanukkah!" He laughed and the others joined in.

When the laughter died down, Jeremy asked, "Can we all sit on the floor and play dreidel? Mom, you and I could sing Grandma the song Caleb taught us."

"How about I bring us some of the yummy donuts to eat while we play?" Mom suggested.

The sounds of singing filled the room. The time passed very quickly, and soon it was time for bed.

Jeremy ran upstairs to get ready. He brushed his teeth, washed his face and hands, and put on his pajamas. He climbed into bed and waited for his bedtime story.

Mom and Dad both came in to say good night, and Grandma sat down in a chair near his bed.

She opened the book and began reading:

Once in ancient Syria,
Lived a cruel and wicked king.
He ruled with hate. He ruled with spite,
Controlling everything!

For all the Jewish people,
Whose children played with dreidels,
He passed a law that everyone
Should only worship idols.

But O the shock, and O the shame
That ran throughout the land!
For these faithful Jewish people,
Loved the God of Abraham.

The wicked king was furious
That he might not have his way.
He did not want these people
To read ... or teach ... or pray.

To make it more impossible
To worship their true God,
He filled their holy Temple
With his unholy gods.

"How mean!" cried Jeremy. "That king shouldn't have told those people not to love God! Right, Grandma?"

"Right, Jeremy," Grandma agreed. "But just listen to what happens next."

That didn't stop the worshippers.
They simply met outside
Until the king sent soldiers
To force them all to hide.

But the children,
with their toy tops,
Turned out to save the day.
When the soldiers came to
halt their talk,
They would pretend to play.

And then one day,
A brave, young Jew—
After years of misery—
Formed a loyal little army;
He was Judah Maccabee.

Even the king's vast army—
No matter how they tried—
Could not beat this tiny fighting force
Because God was on their side!

"Oh, Grandma!" Jeremy blurted out. "That was a real miracle, wasn't it?"

She laid the book on her lap and looked deep into Jeremy's eyes. "Yes, it was a miracle. But never forget, when God is on your side, you don't ever have to be afraid. He always wins!"

Picking up the book again, Grandma continued to read:

Once the Maccabees had won the war,
They hurried to the Temple.
They cleaned it, then they searched for oil,
But it wasn't quite that simple.

The oil was for the Temple lamp,
Which was lit both day and night.
And though they looked both high and low,
It was not anywhere in sight!

At last one soldier spied a vial
Of the pure and precious stuff.
One small bottle, not one drop more!
But would that be enough?

They knew that it would take eight days
For more oil to light the lamp;
So no one knew just what to do —
No one in all the camp.

But then our Great, Almighty God—
We cannot know His ways!—
Made those few drops of holy oil
Last for all eight days!

Now Jeremy's eyes were wide. "Wow, Gram," he said quietly. "I guess God likes to work miracles."

Grandma closed the book. "Yes, Jeremy, He does. This is the beautiful story telling why the Jewish people celebrate Hanukkah and why they have a Hanukkiah with nine candles— to remember the eight days the oil lasted—and one more candle to light them all.

"Jeremy, while the story is beautiful, we can't prove it happened quite like this, so it is called a legend. Let me tell you what we learned from history.

"History records that once Judah's army took back the Temple from the King's men and cleaned it up, they decided to keep a special eight-day celebration called Tabernacles or Feasts of Booths. Long before this war Moses recorded God's instructions about how to celebrate tabernacles in the Bible.

"Jeremy, the first time we hear about the word tabernacle is when the Jewish people came out of Egypt and God told them to build a tabernacle so He could meet with them. It was called the tent of meeting.

"God told Moses, 'tell the Jewish people, every year, make a temporary dwelling to live in for eight days.' Today they call that dwelling a Sukkah. God wanted the Jewish people always to remember He was with them when He took them out of Egypt and away from a mean Pharaoh. Just like God was with the Jewish people and got them away from the mean King Antiochus.

"Tabernacles was also a time to celebrate the harvest and remember God's blessing to provide for them. Even though Tabernacles happens in the fall season, the Maccabees decided to have that celebration when they got the temple back in December.

"What is so interesting about that, Jeremy, is we have found clues in the Bible that tell us Jesus was really born at tabernacles, which is in the fall.

"Even though most of the world celebrates Jesus' birthday in December, which is when the Maccabees took the temple back, the Bible reveals a mystery about the timing of Jesus' birth. The mystery clue is hidden in the statement that when the angel came to Mary, he told her Elizabeth was six months pregnant.

"Jesus really did come to earth in December when Mary became pregnant by the Holy Spirit, but he was born in the fall season of tabernacles. There are other clues we can talk about another time.

"God is so good that He made sure that if some people want to celebrate Jesus in December, it was the time Jesus came to the earth. If some people celebrate at Tabernacles, that was the time Jesus was revealed to the world.

"The most important thing is that people celebrate Jesus, God's greatest gift to us. Jesus was born in the season when God was telling the people, 'Remember I am with you.'

"Jeremy, what the Maccabees did was so important because God's plan was that Jesus was to be Jewish and if King Antiochus had won, there would have been no Jewish people left. This story shows us God's plans never fail.

"Since Jesus is Jewish, when He was on earth, he celebrated Hanukkah. You can read about it in the book of John. They called it at that time, the Feast of Dedication.

"Jeremy, here's a picture of what one of my friends does. They combined both the time Mary became pregnant with Jesus and the time He was born. The Sukkah in their living room, reminds them of the time when Jesus was born, the Christmas ornaments hung on the Sukkah remind them of when Mary was pregnant."

"Caleb's mom said that Hanukkah means dedication. They celebrate the dedication of the temple. Gram, what does dedication mean?" questioned Jeremy.

"Well, let's see if I can explain it to you, Jeremy. What they did is pray and thank God for giving them back their temple. They told God that this place was for Him and it would always be a place they would come to sing, pray, and learn about Him.

"That is why it was so important that God helped them get back God's Temple, so they could keep honoring God and teaching others about Him.

"There is one sad part of this story. Many Jewish people today do not know Jesus is their Messiah. Messiah is the Jewish word for savior.

"You know Jeremy, when I was very young I grew up the only Jewish girl in my town. A neighbor shared Bible stories with me. I found out that Jesus died for me and if I believed that and asked Him into my heart, I could have eternal life with God. I am so happy that she did. When I first found out Jesus was my Savior, I didn't realize how important it was that He was my Jewish Messiah.

"I did not teach my children about the Jewishness of Jesus. It wasn't until I got much older that I understood and now I can teach you and others.

"Jeremy now we are the temple of the Lord. At Hanukkah time when we light the candles we can be grateful for what God has done for us through Jesus. As we light the Hanukkah lights we can remember His love and ask Him to help us be a light to the world to show others God's love."

"I have been thinking, Grandma, God, has never stopped working miracles, has He?" Jeremy's eyes were shining.

"It was a miracle when Judah's small army beat the king's big army, and that a little bit of oil lasted a whole week! It was a miracle when God sent a Baby to save the whole world! Gram, I want to thank God in a special way for all His miracles. I want to be a light, too, and share His love with everyone!" Jeremy said, spreading his arms wide.

Grandma smiled. "Jeremy, that is wonderful! This year, we can remember all God has done for us in a new way. Now that we have our own Hanukkiah, along with the lights on our Christmas tree, why don't we light the Hanukkah candles and have our own Celebration of Lights? Since now we are the temple, when we light the lights, we can say a prayer to dedicate ourselves to God's will to share His love, and we can thank Him for Hanukkah that saved the Jewish people so Jesus could be born."

"Yes, let's do that," said Jeremy. "This year, while Caleb's family celebrates the Festival of Lights, we will celebrate the birthday of Jesus. We know Jesus is the light of the world that gives us eternal life, and did you know they call the light in their temple the Eternal Light? So, Grandma, let's pray that Caleb's family will someday learn that Jesus is their Eternal Light, just like you did."

"Jeremy, I think that's a wonderful idea." Grandma smiled and kissed him good night.

Melody Hope was a storyteller long before she became an author. Her books and family fun ideas came out of her passion to make each day a celebration of learning for her own children and eventually her grandchildren. In time, she opened her doors to her community and created a daycare full of the stories and activities you find in her books. Her deep desire is to see every child have the opportunity to grow up with character, creativity and confidence.

Laurie Wong's love for animals led her to encounter Jesus through CS Lewis' writings. She is a mother of 4, Grandmother of 9 wonderful children and spiritual mom to as many as God brings to the farm she shares with her husband Stuart. Art is just one of the expressions she employs to express the love of Jesus.

Also available in the *The Jeremy Series....*

The Birthday Quilt

Jeremy's birthday has arrived and this birthday is special because he's moving from his crib to his first big-boy bed. *The Birthday Quilt* is a heartwarming story filled with the sounds of life, the excitement of transition and a special mystery. Extra bonus family fun guide accompanies this book with projects the whole family can enjoy.

Thank You Saturday

What are you thankful for? How do you bless others? Join Jeremy's family as they put principle into practice and open their home to a family in need. Faith meets works, creating hope in *Thank You Saturday*. Family fun guide included.

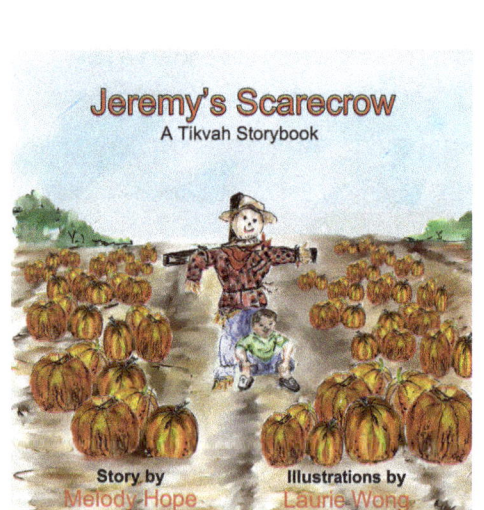

Jeremy's Scarecrow

Jeremy's Scarecrow is a story written for you and your child to explore the importance and rewards of friendship and the need for patience while learning to wait. This book also contains a family fun guide with a project the whole family will enjoy.

New Series to Look Forward to

Friendship Forest Series

In this series, Grandma Owl shares exciting adventures that teach your child about the gifts and callings in the body of Christ. The author shares the true adventures of her friends who walk with Jesus in the pulpit, mission field, or marketplace. Every book ends with an invitation to the reader to go on their own adventure by giving their heart to Jesus. The author's friends are characterized as animals for your children's delight.

This new series' first book tells how Friendship Forest got its name and introduces Grandma Owl, the Friendship Forest storyteller, and Kedrick, the lovable dog who found his new home with Grandma Owl's help.

Dear reader may I also invite you to my ministry website:

WWW.OIMM.ORG

Here you will find teaching from a Hebraic Perspective by Joan Masterson/Melody Hope and many seasoned teachers and authors, as well as a book review section and introductions to many ministries that carry the heart of this author.

For more Hanukkah stories, go to the Children's page
http://www.oimm.org/blog-childrens-section/

Adult in depth teaching on Hanukkah and the Menorah can be found at
http://www.oimm.org/blog-hanukkah/

Also available....

Dwelling PLACE

God's Endtime Strategy
A Dwelling Place for Himself
in the Hearts
of His Sons and Daughters

Dwelling Place is a must read for anyone who is trying to figure out where they fit in God's big plan. He longs for sons and daughters to come home to sit at His table and learn of His ways.

Written from the heart of a Jewish believer who has lived through her identity crisis, this book brings understanding as it delivers a very real picture of Ephesian's "One New Man," — the dwelling place of God in the Spirit among His Jewish and Gentile children.

———

The Jeremy Series by Melody Hope and The Dwelling Place by Joan Masterson can be purchased at Amazon.com, BarnesandNoble.com, Walmart.com and Target.com.

www.ingramcontent.com/pod-product-compliance
Lightning Source LLC
Chambersburg PA
CBHW061149010526
44118CB00026B/2919